Inner Reflections

2010 Engagement Calendar

SELECTIONS FROM THE WRITINGS OF
PARAMAHANSA YOGANANDA

SELF-REALIZATION FELLOWSHIP

FRONT COVER:
Lupines, Redwood National Park, California
Photograph by Mary Liz Austin
Design by Santiago Herrera, Jr.

NOTE: *Holidays and other observed dates are included for the United States (U.S.), Canada,*
England (Eng.), Wales, Scotland (Scot.), Australia (Aus.), and New Zealand (N.Z.).
In addition, moon phases and any eclipses are based on U.S.A. Pacific time.

Printed in Verona, Italy, by EBS
4800-J999

The scenery of mountains painted on the ever-changing
azure canvas of the sky, the mysterious mechanism
of the human body, the rose, the green grass carpet,
the magnanimity of souls, the loftiness of minds,
the depth of love—all these things remind us of a God
who is beautiful and noble.

—*Paramahansa Yogananda*

~

THE PHOTOGRAPHS IN THIS CALENDAR are accompanied by selections from the writings of Paramahansa Yogananda, whose timeless and universal teachings have awakened many, of all races, cultures, and creeds, to a deeper awareness of the one reality that sustains and unites us all.

Whether spread over the vast heavens or hidden in the exquisite delicacy of a tiny flower, nature's beauty is always beckoning, inviting us to look behind the outward form and sense the presence of God within.

We hope that the thoughts and images in these pages will bring you inspiration and encouragement in the days and weeks of the coming year.

Lupines, Redwood National Park, California   Photograph by Mary Liz Austin

$\mathcal{B}$eginning with the early dawn each day, I will radiate
joy to everyone I meet….Before the unfading light
of my cheer, darkness will take flight.

— *Paramahansa Yogananda*

Vermillion Lake, Alberta, Canada   Photograph by Marc Adamus

- I am safe
- Look out for Jade, she is lost.

28 monday

- It's hard to let go.
- Just let go & live my life.
- Enjoy each moment

29 tuesday

- Need to start looking after myself.
- start power thinking at least once a week
- write thoughts out.
- I sleep well & fully each night

30 wednesday

- Be safe
- Be happy
- Be present

31 thursday

- New beginnings
- Choose wisely

1 friday

New Year's Day

- What you want can be achieved.
- Think Big

2 saturday

- Fill myself up with light
- All is ok

3 sunday

January

4
monday

Bank Holiday (Scot.)   Day After New Year's Day (N.Z.)

5
tuesday

Paramahansa Yogananda's Birthday

6
wednesday

7
thursday

Last Quarter ◑

8
friday

9
saturday

			January			
s	m	t	w	t	f	s
					1	2
3	4	5	6	7	8	9
10	11	12	13	14	15	16
17	18	19	20	21	22	23
24 31	25	26	27	28	29	30

			February			
s	m	t	w	t	f	s
	1	2	3	4	5	6
7	8	9	10	11	12	13
14	15	16	17	18	19	20
21	22	23	24	25	26	27
28						

10
sunday

𝒯hrough meditation one can experience a stable, silent inner peace that can be a permanently soothing background for all harmonious or trialsome activities demanded by life's responsibilities.

— Paramahansa Yogananda

Grist Mill, Babcock State Park, West Virginia   Photograph by Daybreak Images

Calm the mind, that without distortion it may mirror Omnipresence.

— *Paramahansa Yogananda*

Mt. Shuksan in Picture Lake, Washington   Photograph by Shaun Cunningham

11
monday

12
tuesday

13
wednesday

14
thursday

15
friday

New Moon ●

January

s	m	t	w	t	f	s
					1	2
3	4	5	6	7	8	9
10	11	12	13	14	15	16
17	18	19	20	21	22	23
24₃₁	25	26	27	28	29	30

16
saturday

February

s	m	t	w	t	f	s
	1	2	3	4	5	6
7	8	9	10	11	12	13
14	15	16	17	18	19	20
21	22	23	24	25	26	27
28						

17
sunday

January

18
monday

Martin Luther King, Jr.'s Birthday (Observed)

19
tuesday

20
wednesday

21
thursday

22
friday

23
saturday

First Quarter ◗

			January			
s	m	t	w	t	f	s
					1	2
3	4	5	6	7	8	9
10	11	12	13	14	15	16
17	18	19	20	21	22	23
24₃₁	25	26	27	28	29	30

			February			
s	m	t	w	t	f	s
	1	2	3	4	5	6
7	8	9	10	11	12	13
14	15	16	17	18	19	20
21	22	23	24	25	26	27
28						

24
sunday

$\mathcal{T}$he wise devotee should be cautious, rather than afraid. He should cultivate a courageous spirit, without rashly exposing himself to conditions that may arouse apprehensions.

— *Paramahansa Yogananda*

Pink anemonefish, Great Barrier Reef, Australia   Photograph by Gary Bell, Oceanwide Images

*T*urn your attention from this world to the kingdom of God which is within.

— *Paramahansa Yogananda*

Polar bears, Hudson's Bay, Canada   Photograph by Tom & Pat Leeson / Kimball Stock

Australia Day (Aus.)

1st Infoceutical taken.
- Heart beat strong in my ears.

2nd dose - ok - heat beat not so strong, in the ears.

3rd dose - Heart doing summersaults, gently but know it
is doing something peculiar.

4th - No probs

January						
s	m	t	w	t	f	s
					1	2
3	4	5	6	7	8	9
10	11	12	13	14	15	16
17	18	19	20	21	22	23
24,31	25	26	27	28	29	30

Full Moon ○

February						
s	m	t	w	t	f	s
	1	2	3	4	5	6
7	8	9	10	11	12	13
14	15	16	17	18	19	20
21	22	23	24	25	26	27
28						

5th - ok

February

1
monday

2
tuesday

3
wednesday

4
thursday

— Feel unwell & slightly off balance lasted for an hr. Then it went.

5
friday

Last Quarter ◑

February

s	m	t	w	t	f	s
	1	2	3	4	5	6
7	8	9	10	11	12	13
14	15	16	17	18	19	20
21	22	23	24	25	26	27
28						

6
saturday

Waitangi Day (N.Z.)

March

s	m	t	w	t	f	s
	1	2	3	4	5	6
7	8	9	10	11	12	13
14	15	16	17	18	19	20
21	22	23	24	25	26	27
28	29	30	31			

7
sunday

$\mathcal{I}$f you always think of God as the nearest of the near,
you will witness many wonders in your life.

— *Paramahansa Yogananda*

When the heart is divinely attuned, close human relationships are opportunities to imbibe God's infinite love from the vessels of many hearts.

— *Paramahansa Yogananda*

Edge of rose petal   Photograph by Charles Needle

8
monday

9
tuesday

10
wednesday

11
thursday

Lincoln's Birthday

12
friday

February

s	m	t	w	t	f	s
		1	2	3	4	5	6
7	8	9	10	11	12	13
14	15	16	17	18	19	20
21	22	23	24	25	26	27
28						

New Moon ●

13
saturday

March

s	m	t	w	t	f	s
		1	2	3	4	5	6
7	8	9	10	11	12	13
14	15	16	17	18	19	20
21	22	23	24	25	26	27
28	29	30	31			

St Valentine's Day (U.S., Canada, and U.K.)

14
sunday

February

15
monday
Washington's Birthday (Observed)   *Presidents' Day*

16
tuesday

17
wednesday

18
thursday

19
friday

20
saturday

February

s	m	t	w	t	f	s
	1	2	3	4	5	6
7	8	9	10	11	12	13
14	15	16	17	18	19	20
21	22	23	24	25	26	27
28						

March

s	m	t	w	t	f	s
	1	2	3	4	5	6
7	8	9	10	11	12	13
14	15	16	17	18	19	20
21	22	23	24	25	26	27
28	29	30	31			

21
sunday
First Quarter ◑

$\mathcal{W}$e should bathe our spirits in the deep, pure feeling that stirs
within us when we gaze on the glories of His creation.
This is the way to know God as beauty.

— *Paramahansa Yogananda*

Lake O'Hara region, British Columbia, Canada   Photograph by Monica Marcu / AKM Images, Inc.

𝒴our countenance should be a beacon for others to follow, a lighthouse by which shipwrecked souls can find the way to safety in the harbor of peace.

— *Paramahansa Yogananda*

Lighthouse, Portland, Maine   Photograph by Cheryl Opperman

February

22
monday

23
tuesday

24
wednesday

25
thursday

26
friday

February

s	m	t	w	t	f	s
	1	2	3	4	5	6
7	8	9	10	11	12	13
14	15	16	17	18	19	20
21	22	23	24	25	26	27
28						

27
saturday

March

s	m	t	w	t	f	s
	1	2	3	4	5	6
7	8	9	10	11	12	13
14	15	16	17	18	19	20
21	22	23	24	25	26	27
28	29	30	31			

Full Moon ○

28
sunday

March

1
monday
St. David's Day (Wales)

2
tuesday

3
wednesday

4
thursday

5
friday

March

s	m	t	w	t	f	s
		1	2	3	4	5	6
7	8	9	10	11	12	13
14	15	16	17	18	19	20
21	22	23	24	25	26	27
28	29	30	31			

6
saturday

April

s	m	t	w	t	f	s
				1	2	3
4	5	6	7	8	9	10
11	12	13	14	15	16	17
18	19	20	21	22	23	24
25	26	27	28	29	30	

7
sunday
Paramahansa Yogananda's Mahasamadhi   Last Quarter ◑

$\mathcal{I}$f you use all available outward means, as well as your natural abilities, to overcome every obstacle in your path, you will thus develop the powers that God gave you—unlimited powers that flow from the innermost forces of your being.

— *Paramahansa Yogananda*

Angel Falls, Venezuela   Photograph by Dave Welling

$\mathcal{A}$ll the ages past are as nothing compared to the eternity of time before you.

— *Paramahansa Yogananda*

Paria Canyon Bowl, Arizona   Photograph by Russ Burden

8
monday

9
tuesday

Sri Yukteswar's Mahasamadhi

10
wednesday

11
thursday

12
friday

March

s	m	t	w	t	f	s
	1	2	3	4	5	6
7	8	9	10	11	12	13
14	15	16	17	18	19	20
21	22	23	24	25	26	27
28	29	30	31			

13
saturday

April

s	m	t	w	t	f	s
				1	2	3
4	5	6	7	8	9	10
11	12	13	14	15	16	17
18	19	20	21	22	23	24
25	26	27	28	29	30	

Daylight Saving Begins (U.S. and Canada)   *Mothering Sunday (Eng.)*

14
sunday

March

15
monday

New Moon ●

16
tuesday

17
wednesday

St. Patrick's Day

18
thursday

19
friday

20
saturday

Vernal Equinox

March

s	m	t	w	t	f	s
		1	2	3	4	5	6
7	8	9	10	11	12	13
14	15	16	17	18	19	20
21	22	23	24	25	26	27
28	29	30	31			

21
sunday

April

s	m	t	w	t	f	s
				1	2	3
4	5	6	7	8	9	10
11	12	13	14	15	16	17
18	19	20	21	22	23	24
25	26	27	28	29	30	

My dreams of perfection are bridges that carry
me into the realm of pure ideas.

— Paramahansa Yogananda

Callaway Gardens, Pine Mountain, Georgia   Photograph by Charles Needle

*T*o develop pure and unconditional love between husband and wife, parent and child, friend and friend, self and all, is the lesson we have come on earth to learn.

— *Paramahansa Yogananda*

Mountain goat and kid, Mt. Evans, Colorado   Photograph by Cathy and Gordon Illg

22
monday

First Quarter ◗

23
tuesday

24
wednesday

25
thursday

26
friday

March

s	m	t	w	t	f	s
	1	2	3	4	5	6
7	8	9	10	11	12	13
14	15	16	17	18	19	20
21	22	23	24	25	26	27
28	29	30	31			

27
saturday

April

s	m	t	w	t	f	s
				1	2	3
4	5	6	7	8	9	10
11	12	13	14	15	16	17
18	19	20	21	22	23	24
25	26	27	28	29	30	

Daylight Saving Begins (U.K. and E U)

28
sunday

March/April

29
monday

Full Moon ○

30
tuesday

Passover Begins

31
wednesday

1
thursday

2
friday

Good Friday

3
saturday

March

s	m	t	w	t	f	s
		1	2	3	4	5	6
7	8	9	10	11	12	13
14	15	16	17	18	19	20
21	22	23	24	25	26	27
28	29	30	31			

4
sunday

April

s	m	t	w	t	f	s
					1	2	3
4	5	6	7	8	9	10
11	12	13	14	15	16	17
18	19	20	21	22	23	24
25	26	27	28	29	30	

Easter Sunday

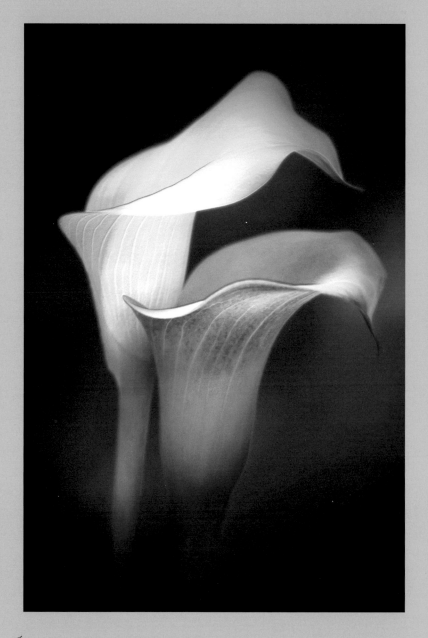

*I*n every lily and in every gentle fragrance you can perceive God's
beauty….He says: "Follow the trail of beauty. I am
hidden somewhere in its heart."

—*Paramahansa Yogananda*

Calla Lilies   Photograph by Ellen Anon

$\mathcal{T}$he sole purpose of creation is to compel you to solve
its mystery and perceive God behind all.

— *Paramahansa Yogananda*

Rhododendron and coast redwoods, Redwood National Park, California   Photograph by Larry Ulrich / Larry Ulrich Stock

5
monday

Easter Monday (All except U.S. and Scot.)

6
tuesday

Last Quarter ◑

7
wednesday

8
thursday

9
friday

April

s	m	t	w	t	f	s
				1	2	3
4	5	6	7	8	9	10
11	12	13	14	15	16	17
18	19	20	21	22	23	24
25	26	27	28	29	30	

10
saturday

May

s	m	t	w	t	f	s
						1
2	3	4	5	6	7	8
9	10	11	12	13	14	15
16	17	18	19	20	21	22
23 30	24 31	25	26	27	28	29

11
sunday

April

12
monday

13
tuesday

14
wednesday

New Moon ●

15
thursday

16
friday

17
saturday

18
sunday

$\mathcal{T}$hose who live in tune with the attractive force of love achieve harmony with nature and their fellow beings.

— *Paramahansa Yogananda*

ℒife is full of bumps and knocks. In the hours of trials, which demand your keenest judgment, if you preserve your mental equilibrium you will attain victory.

— Paramahansa Yogananda

19
monday

20
tuesday

First Quarter ◗

21
wednesday

Earth Day

22
thursday

St. George's Day (Eng.)

23
friday

April

s	m	t	w	t	f	s
				1	2	3
4	5	6	7	8	9	10
11	12	13	14	15	16	17
18	19	20	21	22	23	24
25	26	27	28	29	30	

24
saturday

May

s	m	t	w	t	f	s
						1
2	3	4	5	6	7	8
9	10	11	12	13	14	15
16	17	18	19	20	21	22
23 30	24 31	25	26	27	28	29

ANZAC Day (Aus. and N.Z.)

25
sunday

April/May

26 monday

27 tuesday

28 wednesday

Full Moon ○

29 thursday

30 friday

						April
s	m	t	w	t	f	s
				1	2	3
4	5	6	7	8	9	10
11	12	13	14	15	16	17
18	19	20	21	22	23	24
25	26	27	28	29	30	

1 saturday

National Day of Prayer

						May
s	m	t	w	t	f	s
						1
2	3	4	5	6	7	8
9	10	11	12	13	14	15
16	17	18	19	20	21	22
23 30	24 31	25	26	27	28	29

2 sunday

℮xude peace and goodness; because that is the nature of the
image of God within you—your true nature.

— *Paramahansa Yogananda*

Dahlia petals   Photograph by Charles Needle

$\mathcal{T}$he beauty in the world bespeaks the creative motherly instinct of God, and
when we look upon all the good in Nature, we experience
a feeling of tenderness within us.

— *Paramahansa Yogananda*

May Day Bank Holiday (U.K. and Scot.)

3
monday

4
tuesday

5
wednesday

Last Quarter ◑

6
thursday

7
friday

May

s	m	t	w	t	f	s
						1
2	3	4	5	6	7	8
9	10	11	12	13	14	15
16	17	18	19	20	21	22
23 30	24 31	25	26	27	28	29

8
saturday

June

s	m	t	w	t	f	s
		1	2	3	4	5
6	7	8	9	10	11	12
13	14	15	16	17	18	19
20	21	22	23	24	25	26
27	28	29	30			

Mother's Day (U.S., Canada, Aus., and N.Z.)

9
sunday

May

10
monday

Sri Yukteswar's Birthday

11
tuesday

12
wednesday

13
thursday

New Moon ●

14
friday

					May	
s	m	t	w	t	f	s
						1
2	3	4	5	6	7	8
9	10	11	12	13	14	15
16	17	18	19	20	21	22
23 30	24 31	25	26	27	28	29

15
saturday

					June	
s	m	t	w	t	f	s
		1	2	3	4	5
6	7	8	9	10	11	12
13	14	15	16	17	18	19
20	21	22	23	24	25	26
27	28	29	30			

16
sunday

$\mathcal{L}$ove is the divine power of attraction in creation that
harmonizes, unites, binds together.

— *Paramahansa Yogananda*

Emerald swallowtail butterfly, Washington   Photograph by Darrell Gulin

As the journey of one's existence progresses, one finds by deeper insight into the soul that the quest of life is "Who am I; why am I here?"

— *Paramahansa Yogananda*

May

17
monday

18
tuesday

19
wednesday

First Quarter ◑

20
thursday

21
friday

May

s	m	t	w	t	f	s
						1
2	3	4	5	6	7	8
9	10	11	12	13	14	15
16	17	18	19	20	21	22
23 30	24 31	25	26	27	28	29

22
saturday

June

s	m	t	w	t	f	s
		1	2	3	4	5
6	7	8	9	10	11	12
13	14	15	16	17	18	19
20	21	22	23	24	25	26
27	28	29	30			

23
sunday

May

24
monday

Victoria Day (Canada)

25
tuesday

26
wednesday

27
thursday

Full Moon ○

28
friday

29
saturday

			May			
s	m	t	w	t	f	s
						1
2	3	4	5	6	7	8
9	10	11	12	13	14	15
16	17	18	19	20	21	22
23 30	24 31	25	26	27	28	29

30
sunday

			June			
s	m	t	w	t	f	s
		1	2	3	4	5
6	7	8	9	10	11	12
13	14	15	16	17	18	19
20	21	22	23	24	25	26
27	28	29	30			

$\mathcal{P}$ray that unceasing truth flow into your mind…
and unceasing joy flow into your soul.
— *Paramahansa Yogananda*

Oneonta Falls, Oregon   Photograph by Dennis Frates

$\mathcal{R}$emember only the beautiful things that you have felt, and seen, and experienced. If your five senses behold only the good, then your mind will be a garden of blossoming soul qualities.

— Paramahansa Yogananda

Mt. McGown, Idaho   Photograph by Terry Donnelly

31
monday

Memorial Day   *Spring Bank Holiday (U.K. and Scot.)*

1
tuesday

2
wednesday

3
thursday

4
friday

Last Quarter ◗

May

s	m	t	w	t	f	s
						1
2	3	4	5	6	7	8
9	10	11	12	13	14	15
16	17	18	19	20	21	22
23 30	24 31	25	26	27	28	29

5
saturday

June

s	m	t	w	t	f	s
		1	2	3	4	5
6	7	8	9	10	11	12
13	14	15	16	17	18	19
20	21	22	23	24	25	26
27	28	29	30			

6
sunday

June

7
monday

Queen's Birthday (N.Z.)

8
tuesday

9
wednesday

10
thursday

11
friday

			June			
s	m	t	w	t	f	s
		1	2	3	4	5
6	7	8	9	10	11	12
13	14	15	16	17	18	19
20	21	22	23	24	25	26
27	28	29	30			

12
saturday

New Moon ●

			July			
s	m	t	w	t	f	s
				1	2	3
4	5	6	7	8	9	10
11	12	13	14	15	16	17
18	19	20	21	22	23	24
25	26	27	28	29	30	31

13
sunday

$\mathcal{D}$roplets of love sparkle in true souls, but in Spirit
alone is found the sea of love.

— Paramahansa Yogananda

Water drops on nasturtium leaf   Photograph by Tom Woltjer

Whom God protects, nothing can destroy.

— *Paramahansa Yogananda*

Tiger cub   Photograph by Juniors Bildarchiv / Photolibrary

14
monday

Queen's Birthday (Aus.)

15
tuesday

16
wednesday

17
thursday

18
friday

June

s	m	t	w	t	f	s
		1	2	3	4	5
6	7	8	9	10	11	12
13	14	15	16	17	18	19
20	21	22	23	24	25	26
27	28	29	30			

First Quarter ◐

19
saturday

July

s	m	t	w	t	f	s
				1	2	3
4	5	6	7	8	9	10
11	12	13	14	15	16	17
18	19	20	21	22	23	24
25	26	27	28	29	30	31

Father's Day (U.S., Canada, and U.K.)

20
sunday

June

21
monday

Summer Solstice

22
tuesday

23
wednesday

24
thursday

25
friday

26
saturday

Full Moon ○

			June			
s	m	t	w	t	f	s
		1	2	3	4	5
6	7	8	9	10	11	12
13	14	15	16	17	18	19
20	21	22	23	24	25	26
27	28	29	30			

27
sunday

			July			
s	m	t	w	t	f	s
				1	2	3
4	5	6	7	8	9	10
11	12	13	14	15	16	17
18	19	20	21	22	23	24
25	26	27	28	29	30	31

𝒴our physical eyes show you only a very limited scope of light, but your
spiritual astral eye sees the true nature of all things as
images composed of God's creative light.

— *Paramahansa Yogananda*

"Kent Beauty" oregano   Photograph by Don Paulson

*A*ll the power you use—to think, to speak, and to act—comes from God....
As soon as you actually realize that, a flash of illumination
will come and fear will leave you.

— *Paramahansa Yogananda*

Lightning, Mt. Rainier National Park, Washington   Photograph by LindaDrake.com

28
monday

29
tuesday

30
wednesday

Canada Day (Canada)

1
thursday

2
friday

June

s	m	t	w	t	f	s
		1	2	3	4	5
6	7	8	9	10	11	12
13	14	15	16	17	18	19
20	21	22	23	24	25	26
27	28	29	30			

3
saturday

July

s	m	t	w	t	f	s
				1	2	3
4	5	6	7	8	9	10
11	12	13	14	15	16	17
18	19	20	21	22	23	24
25	26	27	28	29	30	31

Independence Day   *Last Quarter* ◑

4
sunday

July

5
monday

6
tuesday

7
wednesday

8
thursday

9
friday

10
saturday

July

s	m	t	w	t	f	s
				1	2	3
4	5	6	7	8	9	10
11	12	13	14	15	16	17
18	19	20	21	22	23	24
25	26	27	28	29	30	31

August

s	m	t	w	t	f	s
1	2	3	4	5	6	7
8	9	10	11	12	13	14
15	16	17	18	19	20	21
22	23	24	25	26	27	28
29	30	31				

11
sunday

New Moon ●

$\mathcal{Y}$ou cannot remain stationary. You must go either forward or backward.

— *Paramahansa Yogananda*

*B*y seeking goodness, being good, and affirming good,
you see this world as a garden of beauty.

— *Paramahansa Yogananda*

Briones Regional Park, California   Photograph by Gary Crabbe

12
monday

13
tuesday

14
wednesday

15
thursday

16
friday

July

s	m	t	w	t	f	s
				1	2	3
4	5	6	7	8	9	10
11	12	13	14	15	16	17
18	19	20	21	22	23	24
25	26	27	28	29	30	31

17
saturday

August

s	m	t	w	t	f	s
1	2	3	4	5	6	7
8	9	10	11	12	13	14
15	16	17	18	19	20	21
22	23	24	25	26	27	28
29	30	31				

First Quarter ◑

18
sunday

July

19
monday

20
tuesday

21
wednesday

22
thursday

23
friday

24
saturday

		July				
s	m	t	w	t	f	s
				1	2	3
4	5	6	7	8	9	10
11	12	13	14	15	16	17
18	19	20	21	22	23	24
25	26	27	28	29	30	31

		August				
s	m	t	w	t	f	s
1	2	3	4	5	6	7
8	9	10	11	12	13	14
15	16	17	18	19	20	21
22	23	24	25	26	27	28
29	30	31				

25
sunday

Mahavatar Babaji Commemoration Day   Full Moon ○

With calculated precision God has ordained the structural form of each living thing….What tremendous intelligence is manifested in creation!

— *Paramahansa Yogananda*

Hobblebush leaf   Photograph by Sven Halling

$\mathcal{T}$he divine philosopher is the truly happy man....He peers through
the windows of ever-changing physical forms and
beholds God's changeless beauty.

— *Paramahansa Yogananda*

Painted Hills National Monument, Oregon   Photograph by Marc Adamus

26
monday

27
tuesday

28
wednesday

29
thursday

30
friday

July

s	m	t	w	t	f	s
				1	2	3
4	5	6	7	8	9	10
11	12	13	14	15	16	17
18	19	20	21	22	23	24
25	26	27	28	29	30	31

31
saturday

August

s	m	t	w	t	f	s
1	2	3	4	5	6	7
8	9	10	11	12	13	14
15	16	17	18	19	20	21
22	23	24	25	26	27	28
29	30	31				

1
sunday

August

2
monday
Summer Bank Holiday (Scot.)

3
tuesday
Last Quarter ◗

4
wednesday

5
thursday

6
friday

August

s	m	t	w	t	f	s
1	2	3	4	5	6	7
8	9	10	11	12	13	14
15	16	17	18	19	20	21
22	23	24	25	26	27	28
29	30	31				

7
saturday

September

s	m	t	w	t	f	s
			1	2	3	4
5	6	7	8	9	10	11
12	13	14	15	16	17	18
19	20	21	22	23	24	25
26	27	28	29	30		

8
sunday

To be calmly active and actively calm—a Prince of Peace
sitting on the throne of poise, directing the kingdom
of activity—is to be spiritually healthy.

— *Paramahansa Yogananda*

Mountain lion, Wildlife Waystation, California   Photograph by Dave Welling

$\mathcal{B}$ecome one with the Divine Sculptor and make of
your destiny whatever you want it to be.

— *Paramahansa Yogananda*

Spider Rock, Canyon de Chelly, Arizona   Photograph by Tom Vezo

9
monday

New Moon ●

10
tuesday

11
wednesday

12
thursday

13
friday

August

s	m	t	w	t	f	s
1	2	3	4	5	6	7
8	9	10	11	12	13	14
15	16	17	18	19	20	21
22	23	24	25	26	27	28
29	30	31				

14
saturday

September

s	m	t	w	t	f	s
			1	2	3	4
5	6	7	8	9	10	11
12	13	14	15	16	17	18
19	20	21	22	23	24	25
26	27	28	29	30		

15
sunday

August

16
monday

17
tuesday

18
wednesday

19
thursday

20
friday

August

s	m	t	w	t	f	s
1	2	3	4	5	6	7
8	9	10	11	12	13	14
15	16	17	18	19	20	21
22	23	24	25	26	27	28
29	30	31				

21
saturday

September

s	m	t	w	t	f	s
				1	2	3	4
5	6	7	8	9	10	11
12	13	14	15	16	17	18
19	20	21	22	23	24	25
26	27	28	29	30		

22
sunday

𝒜man of inspiration is humble....He knows he is a branch of the Divine Vine—that "the branch cannot bear fruit of itself, except it abide in the vine."

— *Paramahansa Yogananda*

Morning glory flowers, San Miguel de Allende, Mexico   Photograph by Nancy Rotenberg

$\mathcal{L}$ive simply and take life more easily. Happiness lies in giving
yourself time to think and to introspect.

— *Paramahansa Yogananda*

23
monday

24
tuesday

Full Moon ○

25
wednesday

26
thursday

27
friday

August

s	m	t	w	t	f	s
1	2	3	4	5	6	7
8	9	10	11	12	13	14
15	16	17	18	19	20	21
22	23	24	25	26	27	28
29	30	31				

28
saturday

September

s	m	t	w	t	f	s
			1	2	3	4
5	6	7	8	9	10	11
12	13	14	15	16	17	18
19	20	21	22	23	24	25
26	27	28	29	30		

29
sunday

August/September

30
monday
 Summer Bank Holiday (U.K. except Scot.)

31
tuesday

1
wednesday
 Last Quarter ◐

2
thursday
 Janmashtami

3
friday

4
saturday

			August			
s	m	t	w	t	f	s
1	2	3	4	5	6	7
8	9	10	11	12	13	14
15	16	17	18	19	20	21
22	23	24	25	26	27	28
29	30	31				

5
sunday
 Father's Day (Aus. and N.Z.)

			September			
s	m	t	w	t	f	s
				1	2	3	4
5	6	7	8	9	10	11
12	13	14	15	16	17	18
19	20	21	22	23	24	25
26	27	28	29	30		

$\mathcal{G}$od is the Cosmic Carpenter who shapes and chisels life into all its forms.

— *Paramahansa Yogananda*

Grandidier Channel, Antarctica   Photograph by John Warburton-Lee / Danita Delimont

There are inconceivable powers locked in the heart of nature—powers that man has yet to discover. And behind all these is a God. There is an Infinite Intelligence that governs all creation.

— *Paramahansa Yogananda*

Augustine Volcano, Alaska   Photograph by Boyd Norton

6
monday

Labor Day (U.S. and Canada)

7
tuesday

8
wednesday

New Moon ●

9
thursday

Rosh Hashanah

10
friday

September

s	m	t	w	t	f	s
			1	2	3	4
5	6	7	8	9	10	11
12	13	14	15	16	17	18
19	20	21	22	23	24	25
26	27	28	29	30		

11
saturday

October

s	m	t	w	t	f	s
					1	2
3	4	5	6	7	8	9
10	11	12	13	14	15	16
17	18	19	20	21	22	23
24 31	25	26	27	28	29	30

12
sunday

September

13
monday

14
tuesday

15
wednesday

First Quarter ◑

16
thursday

17
friday

	September					
s	m	t	w	t	f	s
				1	2	3	4
5	6	7	8	9	10	11
12	13	14	15	16	17	18
19	20	21	22	23	24	25
26	27	28	29	30		

18
saturday

Yom Kippur

	October					
s	m	t	w	t	f	s
					1	2
3	4	5	6	7	8	9
10	11	12	13	14	15	16
17	18	19	20	21	22	23
24 31	25	26	27	28	29	30

19
sunday

If you can stand the challenge of all your trials and
remain calm—that is true happiness.

— *Paramahansa Yogananda*

$\mathcal{D}$etermine now to break out of the jail of habits and race for freedom.

— *Paramahansa Yogananda*

Wild horses, Camargue, France   Photograph by Jim Zuckerman / Kimball Stock

September

20
monday

21
tuesday

U.N. International Day of Peace

22
wednesday

23
thursday

Autumnal Equinox   Full Moon ○

24
friday

September

s	m	t	w	t	f	s
			1	2	3	4
5	6	7	8	9	10	11
12	13	14	15	16	17	18
19	20	21	22	23	24	25
26	27	28	29	30		

25
saturday

October

s	m	t	w	t	f	s
					1	2
3	4	5	6	7	8	9
10	11	12	13	14	15	16
17	18	19	20	21	22	23
24₃₁	25	26	27	28	29	30

Lahiri Mahasaya's Mahasamadhi

26
sunday

September/October

27
monday

28
tuesday

29
wednesday

30
thursday

Lahiri Mahasaya's Birthday   *Last Quarter* ◑

1
friday

2
saturday

3
sunday

September						
s	m	t	w	t	f	s
				1	2	3	4
5	6	7	8	9	10	11
12	13	14	15	16	17	18
19	20	21	22	23	24	25
26	27	28	29	30		

October						
s	m	t	w	t	f	s
					1	2
3	4	5	6	7	8	9
10	11	12	13	14	15	16
17	18	19	20	21	22	23
24 31	25	26	27	28	29	30

*I*n the one perception of God's universal love…stones, trees,
water, earth, all things will embrace you and welcome you
to their one heart-altar of light.

— *Paramahansa Yogananda*

Gunnison Butte, Utah   Photograph by Scott T. Smith

$\mathcal{T}$he soul cannot be confined within man-made boundaries. Its nationality is Spirit; its country is Omnipresence.

— *Paramahansa Yogananda*

Howse Peak, Banff National Park, Canada   Photograph by Larry Ulrich / Larry Ulrich Stock

October

4
monday

5
tuesday

6
wednesday

7
thursday

New Moon ●

8
friday

October

s	m	t	w	t	f	s
					1	2
3	4	5	6	7	8	9
10	11	12	13	14	15	16
17	18	19	20	21	22	23
24 31	25	26	27	28	29	30

9
saturday

November

s	m	t	w	t	f	s
	1	2	3	4	5	6
7	8	9	10	11	12	13
14	15	16	17	18	19	20
21	22	23	24	25	26	27
28	29	30				

10
sunday

October

11
monday

Columbus Day   Thanksgiving Day (Canada)

12
tuesday

13
wednesday

14
thursday

First Quarter ◐

15
friday

16
saturday

October

s	m	t	w	t	f	s
					1	2
3	4	5	6	7	8	9
10	11	12	13	14	15	16
17	18	19	20	21	22	23
24₃₁	25	26	27	28	29	30

November

s	m	t	w	t	f	s
	1	2	3	4	5	6
7	8	9	10	11	12	13
14	15	16	17	18	19	20
21	22	23	24	25	26	27
28	29	30				

17
sunday

The limited human personality can be greatly expanded by meditation….
When your character grows in a spiritual way, you can assume
almost any shade of personality you desire.

— *Paramahansa Yogananda*

Maple, Newhalem, Washington   Photograph by Don Paulson

ℛeflect about God, or about a beautiful peaceful scene, or about some pleasant experience. Calm, positive mental activity is revivifying.

— *Paramahansa Yogananda*

Autumn colors, Vermont   Photograph by Christopher Talbot Frank

October

18
monday

19
tuesday

20
wednesday

21
thursday

22
friday

Full Moon ◯

October

s	m	t	w	t	f	s
					1	2
3	4	5	6	7	8	9
10	11	12	13	14	15	16
17	18	19	20	21	22	23
24 31	25	26	27	28	29	30

November

s	m	t	w	t	f	s
	1	2	3	4	5	6
7	8	9	10	11	12	13
14	15	16	17	18	19	20
21	22	23	24	25	26	27
28	29	30				

23
saturday

24
sunday

October

25
monday

26
tuesday

27
wednesday

28
thursday

29
friday

Courage & Power night

30
saturday

Symbolises the bull's
horns a sign of
Power.

Last Quarter ◑

- make a commitment to move
forward fearlessly.
Ask Archangel Michael to boost

31
sunday

my courage to take steps to manifest my
lifes purpose.

October						
s	m	t	w	t	f	s
					1	2
3	4	5	6	7	8	9
10	11	12	13	14	15	16
17	18	19	20	21	22	23
24/31	25	26	27	28	29	30

November						
s	m	t	w	t	f	s
	1	2	3	4	5	6
7	8	9	10	11	12	13
14	15	16	17	18	19	20
21	22	23	24	25	26	27
28	29	30				

From that sphere where the mind cannot penetrate, God is pouring
forth His essential Light—the Cosmic Intelligent Vibration
that structures finite creation.

— *Paramahansa Yogananda*

Open your eyes and see the good that you now have, and then keep alert and alive to recognize each new manifestation as it comes to you.

— *Paramahansa Yogananda*

English Kingfisher, Hessen, Germany　　Photograph by Horst Helvik / SpectrumPhotoFile

1 monday

2 tuesday

General Election Day

Meditate about my desires, tell the ~~that~~ dark moon of my intentions.

3 wednesday

(saying how I have already achieved my desires)

4 thursday

Ask the new moon & Archangel Haniel to guide my actions in manifesting these intentions & affirm that they work out for the highest good.

5 friday

Guy Fawkes Day (Eng.)

November

s	m	t	w	t	f	s
	1	2	3	4	5	6
7	8	9	10	11	12	13
14	15	16	17	18	19	20
21	22	23	24	25	26	27
28	29	30				

New Moon ●

Manifesting Night

6 saturday

December

s	m	t	w	t	f	s
			1	2	3	4
5	6	7	8	9	10	11
12	13	14	15	16	17	18
19	20	21	22	23	24	25
26	27	28	29	30	31	

Daylight Saving Ends (U.S. and Canada)

7 sunday

November

8
monday

9
tuesday

On this evening, make a commitment to move forward fearlessly.

10
wednesday

Ask Archangel Michael to boost my courage to take steps to manifest my life's purpose.

11
thursday

12
friday

Courage & Power

13
saturday

First Quarter ◐

November
s	m	t	w	t	f	s
	1	2	3	4	5	6
7	8	9	10	11	12	13
14	15	16	17	18	19	20
21	22	23	24	25	26	27
28	29	30				

December
s	m	t	w	t	f	s
			1	2	3	4
5	6	7	8	9	10	11
12	13	14	15	16	17	18
19	20	21	22	23	24	25
26	27	28	29	30	31	

14
sunday

May we reach our Home by following the inner light—intuition.

— *Paramahansa Yogananda*

𝒴ou should look at life unmasked, in the mirror of your experiences....
Look at the perpetual current of emotions and thoughts that
arise within you....Seek understanding with your highest
intelligence, wisdom, love, and vision.

— *Paramahansa Yogananda*

Bond Falls, Michigan   Photograph by Steve Gettle

Full Moon
Releasing night

When it is completely full

Give the moon everything
   that I want to release.

OR
- write then burn
- Mentally release.

November

15
monday

16
tuesday

17
wednesday

18
thursday

19
friday

20
saturday

21
sunday

November

s	m	t	w	t	f	s
		1	2	3	4	5	6
7	8	9	10	11	12	13
14	15	16	17	18	19	20
21	22	23	24	25	26	27
28	29	30				

December

s	m	t	w	t	f	s
			1	2	3	4
5	6	7	8	9	10	11
12	13	14	15	16	17	18
19	20	21	22	23	24	25
26	27	28	29	30	31	

Full Moon ○

Evening Prior
- Recharging night

November

22
monday

23
tuesday

24
wednesday

25
thursday

Thanksgiving Day

26
friday

27
saturday

Couvape & Power

November

s	m	t	w	t	f	s
		1	2	3	4	5	6
7	8	9	10	11	12	13
14	15	16	17	18	19	20
21	22	23	24	25	26	27
28	29	30				

December

s	m	t	w	t	f	s
			1	2	3	4
5	6	7	8	9	10	11
12	13	14	15	16	17	18
19	20	21	22	23	24	25
26	27	28	29	30	31	

28
sunday

Last Quarter ◗

*W*herever you are, there you must win your victory.
You do not win by flying away or giving up.

— *Paramahansa Yogananda*

Northern cardinal, Brighton, Michigan   Photograph by Steve Gettle

*I*n the airplane of your visualization, glide over the limitless empire
of thoughts. There behold the mountain ranges of
unbroken, lofty, spiritual aspirations.

— *Paramahansa Yogananda*

Gesaeuse, Austria   Photograph by Christian Jungwirth / www.bigshot.at

29
monday

30
tuesday

St. Andrew's Day (Scot.)

1
wednesday

2
thursday

Hanukkah

3
friday

December

s	m	t	w	t	f	s
			1	2	3	4
5	6	7	8	9	10	11
12	13	14	15	16	17	18
19	20	21	22	23	24	25
26	27	28	29	30	31	

4
saturday

January 2011

s	m	t	w	t	f	s
						1
2	3	4	5	6	7	8
9	10	11	12	13	14	15
16	17	18	19	20	21	22
23 30	24 31	25	26	27	28	29

Manifesting Night

New Moon ●

5
sunday

December

6
monday

7
tuesday

8
wednesday

9
thursday

10
friday

11
saturday

12
sunday

December

s	m	t	w	t	f	s
			1	2	3	4
5	6	7	8	9	10	11
12	13	14	15	16	17	18
19	20	21	22	23	24	25
26	27	28	29	30	31	

January 2011

s	m	t	w	t	f	s
						1
2	3	4	5	6	7	8
9	10	11	12	13	14	15
16	17	18	19	20	21	22
23 30	24 31	25	26	27	28	29

𝒮ife was given that we might find the Eternal Life. Peace
was given that we might find the Eternal Peace.

— *Paramahansa Yogananda*

South Berwick, Maine   Photograph by Larry Landolfi / Photo Researchers, Inc.

$\mathcal{E}$very person needs a retreat, a dynamo of silence where he may go for the exclusive purpose of being recharged by the Infinite.

— *Paramahansa Yogananda*

Winter scene, Manitoba, Canada   Photograph by Mike Grandmaison

Power & courage .

First Quarter ◐

13
monday

14
tuesday

15
wednesday

16
thursday

17
friday

December

s	m	t	w	t	f	s
				1	2	3	4
5	6	7	8	9	10	11
12	13	14	15	16	17	18
19	20	21	22	23	24	25
26	27	28	29	30	31	

18
saturday

January 2011

s	m	t	w	t	f	s
						1
2	3	4	5	6	7	8
9	10	11	12	13	14	15
16	17	18	19	20	21	22
23 30	24 31	25	26	27	28	29

19
sunday

December

20
monday

21
tuesday

Releasing Night

Winter Solstice   Full Moon ○

22
wednesday

23
thursday

24
friday

25
saturday

Christmas Day

December

s	m	t	w	t	f	s
			1	2	3	4
5	6	7	8	9	10	11
12	13	14	15	16	17	18
19	20	21	22	23	24	25
26	27	28	29	30	31	

January 2011

s	m	t	w	t	f	s
						1
2	3	4	5	6	7	8
9	10	11	12	13	14	15
16	17	18	19	20	21	22
23 30	24 31	25	26	27	28	29

26
sunday

Boxing Day (Canada, U.K., Aus., and N.Z.)

Christ came to bring you joy, and glory, and peace, and light.
These he offers to you always, but with especial
tenderness and love at this holy season.

— *Paramahansa Yogananda*

Sunset Trophy Mountains, Canada   Photograph by Alan Fortune / Animals Animals

$\mathcal{B}$ehold, through the gates of the New Year, the distant variegated
decorations of future achievements glimmering at you
and daringly luring you to give pursuit.

— *Paramahansa Yogananda*

Sunrise on Torres del Paine, Chile   Photograph by Howie Garber

Power & Courage

Christmas Holiday (Canada, Aus., N.Z. – observed)   Bank Holiday (U.K.)

Last Quarter ◐

27
monday

Boxing Day Holiday (Canada, Aus., N.Z. – observed)   Bank Holiday (U.K.)

28
tuesday

29
wednesday

30
thursday

31
friday

New Year's Day

December

s	m	t	w	t	f	s
			1	2	3	4
5	6	7	8	9	10	11
12	13	14	15	16	17	18
19	20	21	22	23	24	25
26	27	28	29	30	31	

1
saturday

January 2011

s	m	t	w	t	f	s
						1
2	3	4	5	6	7	8
9	10	11	12	13	14	15
16	17	18	19	20	21	22
23 30	24 31	25	26	27	28	29

2
sunday

ACKNOWLEDGMENTS

∾

We wish to express our sincere appreciation to the following photographers and agencies who contributed to this year's *Inner Reflections* engagement calendar. Following a contributor's name, in parentheses, is the month and a day of the week, or other description, where each photo appears.

Accent Alaska (10/25)

Marc Adamus (12/29/09; 7/26; 11/8)

AKM Images (2/15)

Animals Animals (12/20)

Ellen Anon (3/29)

Mary Liz Austin (Cover; Opening Photo)

Gary Bell, Oceanwide Images (1/18)

www.bigshot.at (11/29)

Craig Blacklock (2/1)

Russ Burden (3/8)

Alan Carey (5/3)

Gary Crabbe (7/12)

Shaun Cunningham (1/11)

Daybreak Images (1/4)

Danita Delimont (8/30)

Terry Donnelly (5/31)

LindaDrake.com (6/28)

Alan Fortune (12/20)

Christopher Talbot Frank (10/18)

Dennis Frates (5/24)

Howie Garber (12/27)

Steve Gettle (11/15; 11/22)

Mike Grandmaison (12/13)

Darrell Gulin (5/10)

Sven Halling (7/19)

Horst Helvik (11/1)

Rolf Hicker (10/25)

Cathy & Gordon Illg (3/22)

Christian Jungwirth (11/29)

Kimball Stock (1/25; 7/5; 9/20)

Kitchin & Hurst (7/5)

Larry Landolfi (12/6)

Frans Lanting (5/17)

Tom & Pat Leeson (1/25)

Monica Marcu (2/15)

Charles Needle (2/8; 3/15; 4/26)

Boyd Norton (9/6)

Cheryl Opperman (2/22; 4/19)

Don Paulson (6/21; 10/11)

Photolibrary (6/14)

Photo Researchers, Inc. (5/3; 12/6)

Nancy Rotenberg (8/16)

Ron Sanford (8/23)

Scott T. Smith (9/27)

Spantrans (9/13)

SpectrumPhotoFile (11/1)

SuperStock, Inc. (9/13)

Larry Ulrich Stock (2/1; 4/5; 10/4)

Tom Vezo (8/9)

John Warburton-Lee (8/30)

Dave Welling (3/1; 8/2)

Art Wolfe (4/12)

Tom Woltjer (6/7)

Jim Zuckerman (9/20)

PARAMAHANSA YOGANANDA
1893–1952

BORN IN NORTHERN INDIA IN 1893, Paramahansa Yogananda came to the United States in 1920 as a delegate to an international congress of religious leaders convening in Boston. He remained in the West for the better part of the next thirty-two years, until his passing in 1952. Reporting at that time on his life and work, a Los Angeles periodical wrote: "Yogananda made an outstanding cultural and spiritual contribution in furthering the cause of better understanding between East and West. He combined in a conspicuous degree the spiritual idealism of India with practical activity of the West....The centers he established, the great numbers he inspired to nobler living, and the ideals he planted in the common consciousness of humanity will ever remain a monument to his notable achievement."

Self-Realization Fellowship, the international nonprofit society founded by Paramahansa Yogananda in 1920, is dedicated to carrying on his spiritual and humanitarian work — fostering a spirit of greater harmony and understanding among those of all nations and faiths, and introducing to truth-seekers all over the world his universal teachings on the ancient science of Yoga.

Paramahansa Yogananda's life story, *Autobiography of a Yogi,* is considered a modern spiritual classic. It has been translated into more than twenty languages and is widely used in college and university courses. A perennial best seller since it was first published more than sixty years ago, the book has found its way into the hearts of readers around the world.

An introductory booklet about the life and teachings of Paramahansa Yogananda and a book catalog are available upon request.

SELF-REALIZATION FELLOWSHIP
3880 San Rafael Avenue • Los Angeles, California 90065-3298
Telephone (323) 225-2471 • Fax (323) 225-5088
www.yogananda-srf.org

NOTES

2009

January	February	March	April

January

s	m	t	w	t	f	s
				1	2	3
4	5	6	7	8	9	10
11	12	13	14	15	16	17
18	19	20	21	22	23	24
25	26	27	28	29	30	31

February

s	m	t	w	t	f	s
1	2	3	4	5	6	7
8	9	10	11	12	13	14
15	16	17	18	19	20	21
22	23	24	25	26	27	28

March

s	m	t	w	t	f	s
1	2	3	4	5	6	7
8	9	10	11	12	13	14
15	16	17	18	19	20	21
22	23	24	25	26	27	28
29	30	31				

April

s	m	t	w	t	f	s
			1	2	3	4
5	6	7	8	9	10	11
12	13	14	15	16	17	18
19	20	21	22	23	24	25
26	27	28	29	30		

May

s	m	t	w	t	f	s
					1	2
3	4	5	6	7	8	9
10	11	12	13	14	15	16
17	18	19	20	21	22	23
24,31	25	26	27	28	29	30

June

s	m	t	w	t	f	s
	1	2	3	4	5	6
7	8	9	10	11	12	13
14	15	16	17	18	19	20
21	22	23	24	25	26	27
28	29	30				

July

s	m	t	w	t	f	s
			1	2	3	4
5	6	7	8	9	10	11
12	13	14	15	16	17	18
19	20	21	22	23	24	25
26	27	28	29	30	31	

August

s	m	t	w	t	f	s
						1
2	3	4	5	6	7	8
9	10	11	12	13	14	15
16	17	18	19	20	21	22
23,30	24,31	25	26	27	28	29

September

s	m	t	w	t	f	s
		1	2	3	4	5
6	7	8	9	10	11	12
13	14	15	16	17	18	19
20	21	22	23	24	25	26
27	28	29	30			

October

s	m	t	w	t	f	s
				1	2	3
4	5	6	7	8	9	10
11	12	13	14	15	16	17
18	19	20	21	22	23	24
25	26	27	28	29	30	31

November

s	m	t	w	t	f	s
1	2	3	4	5	6	7
8	9	10	11	12	13	14
15	16	17	18	19	20	21
22	23	24	25	26	27	28
29	30					

December

s	m	t	w	t	f	s
		1	2	3	4	5
6	7	8	9	10	11	12
13	14	15	16	17	18	19
20	21	22	23	24	25	26
27	28	29	30	31		

2011

January

s	m	t	w	t	f	s
						1
2	3	4	5	6	7	8
9	10	11	12	13	14	15
16	17	18	19	20	21	22
23,30	24,31	25	26	27	28	29

February

s	m	t	w	t	f	s
		1	2	3	4	5
6	7	8	9	10	11	12
13	14	15	16	17	18	19
20	21	22	23	24	25	26
27	28					

March

s	m	t	w	t	f	s
		1	2	3	4	5
6	7	8	9	10	11	12
13	14	15	16	17	18	19
20	21	22	23	24	25	26
27	28	29	30	31		

April

s	m	t	w	t	f	s
					1	2
3	4	5	6	7	8	9
10	11	12	13	14	15	16
17	18	19	20	21	22	23
24	25	26	27	28	29	30

May

s	m	t	w	t	f	s
1	2	3	4	5	6	7
8	9	10	11	12	13	14
15	16	17	18	19	20	21
22	23	24	25	26	27	28
29	30	31				

June

s	m	t	w	t	f	s
			1	2	3	4
5	6	7	8	9	10	11
12	13	14	15	16	17	18
19	20	21	22	23	24	25
26	27	28	29	30		

July

s	m	t	w	t	f	s
					1	2
3	4	5	6	7	8	9
10	11	12	13	14	15	16
17	18	19	20	21	22	23
24,31	25	26	27	28	29	30

August

s	m	t	w	t	f	s
	1	2	3	4	5	6
7	8	9	10	11	12	13
14	15	16	17	18	19	20
21	22	23	24	25	26	27
28	29	30	31			

September

s	m	t	w	t	f	s
				1	2	3
4	5	6	7	8	9	10
11	12	13	14	15	16	17
18	19	20	21	22	23	24
25	26	27	28	29	30	

October

s	m	t	w	t	f	s
						1
2	3	4	5	6	7	8
9	10	11	12	13	14	15
16	17	18	19	20	21	22
23,30	24,31	25	26	27	28	29

November

s	m	t	w	t	f	s
		1	2	3	4	5
6	7	8	9	10	11	12
13	14	15	16	17	18	19
20	21	22	23	24	25	26
27	28	29	30			

December

s	m	t	w	t	f	s
				1	2	3
4	5	6	7	8	9	10
11	12	13	14	15	16	17
18	19	20	21	22	23	24
25	26	27	28	29	30	31

2010

January
s	m	t	w	t	f	s
					1	2
3	4	5	6	7	8	9
10	11	12	13	14	15	16
17	18	19	20	21	22	23
24/31	25	26	27	28	29	30

February
s	m	t	w	t	f	s
	1	2	3	4	5	6
7	8	9	10	11	12	13
14	15	16	17	18	19	20
21	22	23	24	25	26	27
28						

March
s	m	t	w	t	f	s
	1	2	3	4	5	6
7	8	9	10	11	12	13
14	15	16	17	18	19	20
21	22	23	24	25	26	27
28	29	30	31			

April
s	m	t	w	t	f	s
				1	2	3
4	5	6	7	8	9	10
11	12	13	14	15	16	17
18	19	20	21	22	23	24
25	26	27	28	29	30	

May
s	m	t	w	t	f	s
						1
2	3	4	5	6	7	8
9	10	11	12	13	14	15
16	17	18	19	20	21	22
23/30	24/31	25	26	27	28	29

June
s	m	t	w	t	f	s
		1	2	3	4	5
6	7	8	9	10	11	12
13	14	15	16	17	18	19
20	21	22	23	24	25	26
27	28	29	30			

July
s	m	t	w	t	f	s
				1	2	3
4	5	6	7	8	9	10
11	12	13	14	15	16	17
18	19	20	21	22	23	24
25	26	27	28	29	30	31

August
s	m	t	w	t	f	s
1	2	3	4	5	6	7
8	9	10	11	12	13	14
15	16	17	18	19	20	21
22	23	24	25	26	27	28
29	30	31				

September
s	m	t	w	t	f	s
			1	2	3	4
5	6	7	8	9	10	11
12	13	14	15	16	17	18
19	20	21	22	23	24	25
26	27	28	29	30		

October
s	m	t	w	t	f	s
					1	2
3	4	5	6	7	8	9
10	11	12	13	14	15	16
17	18	19	20	21	22	23
24/31	25	26	27	28	29	30

November
s	m	t	w	t	f	s
	1	2	3	4	5	6
7	8	9	10	11	12	13
14	15	16	17	18	19	20
21	22	23	24	25	26	27
28	29	30				

December
s	m	t	w	t	f	s
			1	2	3	4
5	6	7	8	9	10	11
12	13	14	15	16	17	18
19	20	21	22	23	24	25
26	27	28	29	30	31	

January

Sunday	Monday	Tuesday	Wednesday	Thursday	Friday	Saturday
					1	2
3	4	5	6	7	8	9
10	11	12	13	14	15	16
17	18	19	20	21	22	23
24	25	26	27	28	29	30
31						

Jan 1   New Year's Day
Jan 4   Day After New Year's Day (N.Z.) / Bank Holiday (Scot.)
Jan 5   Paramahansa Yogananda's Birthday
Jan 18   Martin Luther King, Jr's. Birthday (Observed)
Jan 26   Australia Day (Aus.)

February

Sunday	Monday	Tuesday	Wednesday	Thursday	Friday	Saturday
	1	2	3	4	5	6
7	8	9	10	11	12	13
14	15	16	17	18	19	20
21	22	23	24	25	26	27
28						

Feb 6   Waitangi Day (N.Z.)
Feb 12   Lincoln's Birthday
Feb 14   St. Valentine's Day (U.S., Canada, and U.K.)
Feb 15   Washington's Birthday (Observed) / Presidents' Day

March

Sunday	Monday	Tuesday	Wednesday	Thursday	Friday	Saturday
	1	2	3	4	5	6
7	8	9	10	11	12	13
14	15	16	17	18	19	20
21	22	23	24	25	26	27
28	29	30	31			

Mar 1   St. David's Day (Wales)
Mar 7   Paramahansa Yogananda's Mahasamadhi
Mar 9   Sri Yukteswar's Mahasamadhi
Mar 14 Daylight Saving Begins (U.S. & Canada)
         Mothering Sunday (Eng.)

Mar 17 St. Patrick's Day
Mar 20 Vernal Equinox
Mar 29 Daylight Saving Begins (U.K. &
         European Union)
Mar 30 Passover Begins

April

Sunday	Monday	Tuesday	Wednesday	Thursday	Friday	Saturday
				1	2	3
4	5	6	7	8	9	10
11	12	13	14	15	16	17
18	19	20	21	22	23	24
25	26	27	28	29	30	

Apr 2   Good Friday
Apr 4   Easter Sunday
Apr 5   Easter Monday (All except U.S. and Scot.)
Apr 22   Earth Day

Apr 23   St. George's Day (Eng.)
Apr 25   ANZAC Day (Aus. and N.Z.)

May

Sunday	Monday	Tuesday	Wednesday	Thursday	Friday	Saturday
						1
2	3	4	5	6	7	8
9	10	11	12	13	14	15
16	17	18	19	20	21	22
23	24	25	26	27	28	29
30	31					

May 1 National Day of Prayer
May 3 May Day Bank Holiday (U.K. and Scot.)
May 9 Mother's Day (U.S., Canada, Aus., and N.Z.)
May 10 Sri Yukteswar's Birthday

May 24 Victoria Day (Canada)
May 31 Memorial Day
Spring Bank Holiday (U.K. and Scot.)

June

Sunday	Monday	Tuesday	Wednesday	Thursday	Friday	Saturday
		1	2	3	4	5
6	7	8	9	10	11	12
13	14	15	16	17	18	19
20	21	22	23	24	25	26
27	28	29	30			

June 7   Queen's Birthday (N.Z.)
June 14 Queen's Birthday (Aus.)
June 20 Father's Day (U.S, Canada, and U.K.)
June 21 Summer Solstice

July

Sunday	Monday	Tuesday	Wednesday	Thursday	Friday	Saturday
				1	2	3
4	5	6	7	8	9	10
11	12	13	14	15	16	17
18	19	20	21	22	23	24
25	26	27	28	29	30	31

July 1   Canada Day (Canada)
July 4   Independence Day
July 25   Mahavatar Babaji Commemoration Day

August

Sunday	Monday	Tuesday	Wednesday	Thursday	Friday	Saturday
1	2	3	4	5	6	7
8	9	10	11	12	13	14
15	16	17	18	19	20	21
22	23	24	25	26	27	28
29	30	31				

Aug 2   Summer Bank Holiday (Scot.)
Aug 30   Summer Bank Holiday (U.K. except Scot.)

September

Sunday	Monday	Tuesday	Wednesday	Thursday	Friday	Saturday
			1	2	3	4
5	6	7	8	9	10	11
12	13	14	15	16	17	18
19	20	21	22	23	24	25
26	27	28	29	30		

Sep 2   Janmashtami
Sep 5   Father's Day (Aus. and N.Z.)
Sep 6   Labor Day (U.S. and Canada)
Sep 9   Rosh Hashanah
Sep 18 Yom Kippur

Sep 21 U.N. International Day of Peace
Sep 23 Autumnal Equinox
Sep 26 Lahiri Mahasaya's Mahasamadhi
Sep 30 Lahiri Mahasaya's Birthday

October

Sunday	Monday	Tuesday	Wednesday	Thursday	Friday	Saturday
					1	2
3	4	5	6	7	8	9
10	11	12	13	14	15	16
17	18	19	20	21	22	23
24	25	26	27	28	29	30
31						

Oct 11   Columbus Day
             Thanksgiving Day (Canada)
Oct 25   Labour Day (N.Z.)
Oct 31   Halloween (U.S., Canada, and U.K.)
             Daylight Saving Ends (U.K. and European Union)

November

Sunday	Monday	Tuesday	Wednesday	Thursday	Friday	Saturday
	1	2	3	4	5	6
7	8	9	10	11	12	13
14	15	16	17	18	19	20
21	22	23	24	25	26	27
28	29	30				

Nov 2   General Election Day
Nov 5   Guy Fawkes Day (Eng.)
Nov 7   Daylight Saving Ends (U.S. and Canada)
Nov 11 Veterans Day
        Remembrance Day (Canada)

Nov 14 Remembrance Sunday (U.K.)
Nov 25 Thanksgiving Day
Nov 30 St. Andrew's Day (Scot.)

December

Sunday	Monday	Tuesday	Wednesday	Thursday	Friday	Saturday
			1	2	3	4
5	6	7	8	9	10	11
12	13	14	15	16	17	18
19	20	21	22	23	24	25
26	27	28	29	30	31	

Dec 2   Hanukkah
Dec 21 Winter Solstice
Dec 25 Christmas
Dec 26 Boxing Day (Canada, U.K., Aus., and N.Z.)

NOTES